Laser Racing
Ed Baird

**Photographs by
Tim Hore and Wilson Barnes**

Fernhurst Books

First published 1982 by
Fernhurst Books, 31 Church Road, Hove, East Sussex BN3 2FY

ISBN 0 906754 05 4

Acknowledgements
The photographs for this book were taken by Tim Hore at Queen Mary Sailing Club, Ashford, Middlesex, and by Wilson Barnes in Florida. The photograph on the back cover is reproduced by kind permission of Performance Sailcraft SA, Switzerland; the photographs on this page and on pages 24 and 37 are by Paul Davies, and the photograph on page 17 is by Jeff Martin.

The publishers gratefully acknowledge permission to reproduce the chart on page 27 and the accompanying text which first appeared in Yacht Racing/Cruising Magazine.

The cover design is by Margaret Hallam.

Composition by Allset, London

Printed by Ebenezer Baylis & Son Ltd, Worcester

Printed and bound in Great Britain

Contents

Preparing the boat

I think every sailor I've ever talked to has a different opinion about how often to buy a new boat. Personally, I owned two boats in the first four years that I raced Lasers. The first one I had for about two and a half years. Frankly, the only reason I sold it was because someone offered me nearly the price of a new one for it so I could hardly pass up the deal!

The most important thing you can do is to maintain your boat. Keep it clean and in a bottom cover, and store it inside if possible, making sure that the inside of the hull is dry each time you store it. The major problem most people have with Lasers is that their mast step goes bad after heavy use. This can be prevented, or at least postponed, by stringently cleaning your mast step each time after you go sailing and being sure that before you go out for a sail the mast step is clean and the mast base is also clean. Little particles of sand or dirt, if allowed to accumulate, will quickly tear apart the fiberglass tube that is the main part of your mast step; soon it will begin to leak and soon after that will probably fail.

Generally though a Laser hull should last several years. I've seen people winning large regattas in brand new boats and I've seen them winning in four- and five-year-old boats. Apparently there is little difference in shape or speed as the boat gets older. It's very difficult for a Laser to become soft or weak as it gets older unless it hasn't been cared for properly.

A new boat

When I do get a new boat the first thing I do even before going sailing is to take it to the garage, put it on a pair of sawhorses and unscrew every fitting on the whole boat. Then, using large amounts of silicone sealant around each hole in the boat, I replace all the fittings to their normal position. Some people like to use epoxy for this sealing of the boat but epoxy can crack and then leak, and it can also make replacement or repair of any part nearly impossible.

Next, it's important to install a bailer in your boat. By

following the printed directions very carefully, you can install it in just a few minutes. But be sure you do follow the directions: a badly installed bailer can leak or malfunction.

Spars. Next I like to look at the spars. If these have aluminum rivets holding on the fittings, I replace them with stainless steel or monel rivets. Also the plastic cleats for the traveler, outhaul and cunningham should be replaced immediately with aluminum clam cleats of the same size and design.

Another area to check on your spars is the boom mainsheet blocks. They should probably be bolted through to make sure they don't come apart while you're sailing. This hasn't been a big problem but occasionally a boom block will explode, so check your boom blocks and through-bolt them or use oversized screws to be safe.

Lines. Then I move on to the lines that I'll be using for the boat. The outhaul and cunningham should be 10 feet long; I use 3/16 inch pre-stretched line. The boom vang should be 10 feet long using 5/16 inch pre-stretched. The traveler should be 12 feet long, 5/16 inch in diameter, also pre-stretched. You should also have a bow line of this same length so if your traveler breaks you have a spare. The mainsheet should be 42 feet long, 5/16 inch diameter; use a line that soaks up very little water such as Marstrand or your local equivalent. The clew tie-down should be 15 inches long and 1/8 or 3/16 inch in diameter.

1/8 inch	= 4 or 6 mm
3/16 inch	
5/16 inch	= 8 mm
15 inches	= 38 cm
10 feet	= 3.05 m
12 feet	= 3.65 m
42 feet	= 12.8 m

My fully rigged boat. Note the traveler line and the long tiller extension. The hiking straps are kept off the floor by a loop of elastic.

Right: a cockpit view. Note the boom vang and cunningham rigs. A length of elastic will keep the daggerboard in position when raised; the elastic is tied to keep it clear of the cunningham. Note also the way that all of the mainsheet is kept in front of the feet for less chance of entanglement. The hiking strap is loose enough for the legs to be straight when hiking.

Center, left: note the four-to-one purchase on the cunningham. The boom vang is set up with the cleat next to the boom and with a loop in the rope end for quick access. The bow line is of the proper size and length to be used as a traveler should the traveler break.

Center, right: note the tension put on the clew keeping it right next to the boom. Note also the purchase system on the outhaul, the method of tying the mainsheet and the tape around the traveler blocks which keeps them from binding.

Right: the forward end of the outhaul can be secured around the boom in this fashion, allowing it to be slid forward and aft to keep the line in front of the outhaul cleat out of the skipper's way.

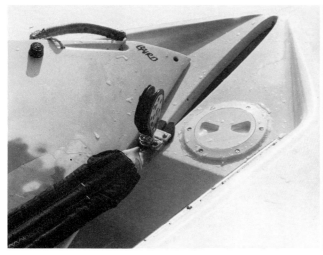

Above, left: on my boat the daggerboard is made easier to pull up by a handle on the top. Note also the padded hiking strap which is bolted through by means of an inspection port to ensure

that it won't pull out of the boat.

Right: the rudder and tiller assembly. Note the extra-large bolt through the head of the rudder, the positioning of the

cleat and the method of attaching the pin to the tiller. Having the tiller cleat very far aft eliminates stretch and extra line from the assembly.

Tiller, rudder and daggerboard. The tiller should be 40 inches long, preferably round so the traveler block slides over it easily. I prefer using a 44-inch tiller extension but an inch or two longer or shorter is a matter of personal preference.

A rope handle should be placed on the top of the dagger-board making it easy to raise and lower around the course (check the class rules to see what is allowed). An elastic cord is required by the class rules to be attached to the front of the daggerboard and to either the mast or the cunningham eye. Mine is only tight when the board is up. On the tiller the downhaul cleat should be moved aft to a position relatively close to the rudder head and just behind the traveler so the rudder down-haul will have less tendency to stretch, which would allow your rudder to lift. On the rudder itself, the head bolt and plastic bushings that come with the standard rudder should be discarded and a larger diameter stainless steel bolt put in their place. The bolt should be as large a diameter as will fit through the hole in the rudder head.

Sail. On the sail I use only one set of telltales placed about 14 inches aft of the luff and in the very lowest panel. I don't use any sort of masthead fly or burgee, relying purely on the tell-

14 inches	= 35 cm
40 inches	= 1.02 m
44 inches	= 1.12 m

7

Setting up the sail controls (*above*). *Left:* for most breezes this configuration is good. Check the outhaul by measuring the distance from the deepest point of the foot of the sail to the boom — this should be three to five inches (8-13 cm) in most winds. The cunningham here is loose and should stay loose until the skipper is overpowered.

Center: here the cunningham is set properly for heavy air but the outhaul has been pulled too tight if, when sailing, the sail looks like this. The sail should never touch the boom at its deepest point while sailing upwind, although it may look as it does here before the sheet has been trimmed in.

Right: this is the position for the cunningham when trimmed for upwind sailing in heavy air. When pulled this tight the cunningham helps to flatten the top of the sail and move the draft forward in the bottom of the sail. The result is more power low down and less power high up in the sail.

tales to help me trim the sail. I think it's important to have a new sail when the present one I'm using is 'getting tired'. Usually, with the amount of racing that I do, a sail will last me a year and a half. Someone who races their Laser every weekend or all season long should probably have a new sail once a year. I probably race an average of one weekend a month all year long and also go to a couple of week-long regattas in the summer.

There's a lot of controversy about picking out masts and sails. I owned three sails over the first four years I raced Lasers and each of them was just what came with the boat or whatever was on the top of the pile at the dealer's shop. In terms of masts, I've never done any testing but I do try and watch out for top sections that are too bendy. If the top of my sail is turned inside out (with lots of horizontal wrinkles) as I sheet the main in all the way the top section is probably too bendy and I'll

My compass and compass bracket. The placement of the compass is important. It should be as far forward as possible while still being visible. If too near the daggerboard, the steel rods that reinforce the daggerboard may affect the compass's ability to help you detect shifts. This positioning seems the best compromise.

I usually sail with just one telltale, positioned as shown.

try to purchase another one that may be a little stronger. But normally the sections that come with the boat are perfectly capable of going fast.

Compass. The compass is something I have found to be extremely helpful. I'm fortunate enough to have acquired a compass built in Sweden by Ansar. I feel that this compass has helped me to gain at least three or four positions in each major regatta I've sailed in since owning it. Two things are important to me when considering a compass. First of all it must be large and easily read and secondly it must be well dampened and not wander back and forth between numbers as you hit waves, something that's vital to Laser sailors. The fitting of the compass is also important. I find the position that I place my compass quite satisfactory; it is located just behind the mast and held onto the boat by the cunningham line as shown in the picture.

Preparing your body

lb		kg
150	=	68
160	=	72
180	=	82
190	=	86

There's really no ideal weight for sailing a Laser although competitive skippers weigh in somewhere between 150 and 190 pounds. Most of the people that can do well in a variety of conditions are between 160 and 180 pounds.

I believe that weight should not be worn when you're racing or practicing. If you're too light to sail a Laser then you should not sail a Laser. Wearing weight can do a lot for you in the short run in terms of being able to hold the boat down for a race or a series or possibly even a number of regattas, but in the long run it's damaging. It's going to hurt your body. It can affect your muscle structure, your posture and it can be very detrimental in terms of back strain and annoyance. Many, many Laser, Finn and other single-handed sailors have experienced lifelong back troubles from wearing too much weight while they were racing. So I feel that wearing weight to increase the boat's stability and increase your hiking power is not advantageous in the long run.

Hiking

As far as training for hiking is concerned, many people set up a hiking bench in their home. I'm sure that's good for them, but personally I've never used one — I feel there is no substitute for getting out in the boat and sailing. However the climate I live in (Florida) enables me to sail any time of the year and therefore I have been able to keep in shape whenever I've wanted. For someone who is not able to sail in the winter, a hiking bench can be part of the answer to staying fit in terms of strength in your legs. Also leg-lifting machines at the health spa can be very helpful for keeping your strength up. But there will still be sore muscles when you go out in the boat and you will have to work for some time to get your legs into shape for hiking, no matter how fit you were over the winter.

When you are sailing you should hike upwind in such a way that you can extend your legs as far as possible while keeping your body as high in the air as you can, giving yourself better leverage on the boat. Move outward as far as possible while

Right: here is the hiking position for medium air. Note the body is in the forward part of the cockpit and feet are hooked under the leeward cockpit rail rather than under the hiking strap.

Center: as the breeze picks up legs should be fully extended by use of the hiking strap so that knees are as close to the edge of the boat as is comfortable. The upper body should then be used to respond to puffs or waves that might make the boat heel to leeward temporarily.

Below, left: this shows the hiking position for a reach, with the legs angled forwards to help take up the slack in the hiking strap and keep the body out of the water.

Below, right: on the run, keep very mobile using your legs to pull you from side to side of the boat. Keep your hands in front of your body and never let go of the mainsheet or tiller.

still feeling comfortable. Bear in mind you've got to hold this position for the entire windward leg. Keep your upper body more or less perpendicular to the water except when you need a little extra power — say in a puff or to hike the boat down over a wave; then extend your upper body for extra leverage. But generally keep your legs as straight as possible, keeping your body out as far as you can, with your upper body vertical.

On the reach, hiking is somewhat different. You're going to be dragging in the water if you hike as you did on the beat. The boat is flatter, the waves are coming up from the side so the strap would work better if it were shortened. Since we can't do that legally, something has to be worked out for the reaches. My technique is to angle my legs from front to back so that my feet are more forward in the boat than my hips. Having your legs angled in such a way takes up the slack of the hiking strap while still allowing you to keep your legs straight and hike hard. When the wind lightens, pull yourself in with your back leg, slightly bending your front leg. Then you're ready to push back out in a puff.

Keeping your boat flat on a run is much easier than sailing to windward or reaching. Very little hiking is required but a large amount of mobility is necessary. You have to keep yourself mobile enough to stop the boat from death rolling to windward while at the same time not letting it heel too far to leeward. Constant adjustment is needed, therefore you have to maintain a posture that places the body *over* the legs. Then, using your legs to pull yourself from one side of the boat to the other can allow you to react quickly to sudden rolls of the boat to windward or to leeward. Also, keeping your hands in front of your body with one hand *always* on the tiller and the other *always*

12

on the mainsheet, will allow you to adjust rapidly to changes in velocity, waves, or both. This is helpful on any leg of the course.

Practice

Practice is something that should be taken extremely seriously by any sailor who's trying to do well. Improving yourself is all-important even if you're already a winner because somebody else is going to try a little bit harder and will outdo you if you are only maintaining your present abilities.

My major advances in ability have come from practicing alone. I just go out and try to make the boat do anything I want. I learn how to tack and gybe and reach and stop and accelerate and sail upwind and downwind as if I were part of the boat. I'm not *making* the boat do things, I am *helping* it do things. I've gone out by myself, rounded markers, done hundreds of tacks in an afternoon, hundreds of gybes, reached for long periods of time, just to *feel* what the boat does and when it feels fast and when it doesn't. I've sailed upwind for long periods of time to get my legs in shape and to achieve a permanent feeling of what the boat does when each particular wave, windshift, or increase or decrease in wind velocity hits it. This is the basis for being able to improve.

It's also important, however, to sail with other groups of boats. The most advantageous way to practice (other than being alone) comes from sailing with one other boat — preferably someone different each time you practice, but it can be helpful even if it's the same person each time. Placing one boat behind the other, sail upwind and try to stay ahead if you're already

Above: sailing in pairs can greatly improve your boat speed. Here is the normal position for starting out on an upwind tuning session. The leeward boat is two boat lengths to leeward and one boat length ahead of the windward boat, not affecting its breeze but close to even as they begin sailing upwind.

Below: Gybing in pairs is also a very effective way to improve boat handling skills. The boat to windward tries to stay in the other boat's wind, forcing it to gybe away as quickly as possible.

ahead or to get ahead if you are behind. This has proven to be one of the best methods I can find for improving my tacks. With the other boat there you are forced to tack in a particular time slot. When he tacks in your wind you have to tack right away to get out. You can't pick your time to tack — you have to do it and do it right or you won't catch up.

The same thing works downwind. Practice gybing and trying to stay right in the other person's wind from behind. When he decides to gybe you have to gybe a little bit faster if you're behind to try to cut across his transom and get into his wind once again. If you're ahead you must try to defend your position.

With two people you can also practice boat speed techniques. I've learned a lot about boat speed by trying small things like pulling the cunningham a little tighter or changing the outhaul position, easing or tightening the vang, sheeting in all the way or easing out a bit. These subtle differences are best learned with one other person. With two or three other people sailing at the same time you are not really able to settle down and concentrate on boat speed because someone is always falling behind or tacking away or forcing another person to tack, and so on.

When you are sailing with three or four people or more, the best thing to practice is tactical situations. Short courses with a tiny starting line are really good. Practice starts, getting ahead at the weather mark and getting inside overlaps at gybe marks and leeward marks. Try to work on controlling as many of the other boats as possible.

So, for boat handling go out on your own, for boat speed and subtle boat-handling techniques go out with one other person, and for tactical practice get as many boats as possible out to practice at once. Of course the latter is the most difficult to organize and the former, practicing by yourself, is the easiest to organize, so probably the main amount of your time will be spent practicing on your own.

Make sure that you don't waste time when you're training. Spend every minute that you're out trying to get better at

something, or resting and contemplating which skill could be improved. Work hard at developing all the things you're going to have to do during a race: tacking, gybing, capsizing and righting the boat, sailing for a long period of time upwind, reaching, straight downwind. Work hard at putting the vang on and off and changing your outhaul and cunningham tensions. Really hustle for a couple of hours and you can get quite a bit accomplished. Do this a couple of days a week, or even one day a week, and you'll quickly improve all of your boat handling and speed needs. *Don't waste time.* Immediately start tacking or gybing on the way out to your course; when you are in a place where you can practice, work hard the whole time that you are there. You'll get a lot more out of the session.

Above: racing with a group of friends on a short course is the best way to practice tactics.

What you do on the morning of a race can greatly affect the outcome of that race, so pay great attention to your preparations. Most important before you leave the dock is to be sure that everything on the boat is in absolutely perfect working order. Sheets should not be frayed, battens should fit correctly into their batten pockets, the compass should be properly affixed, no cleats should be loose, the hiking strap line should be checked, all bolts and screws should be tightened, and rivets and other fastenings should be looked over. Remember your protest flag and lifejacket, too.

On the way out to the course pay careful attention to changing conditions, any detectable windshifts, changes in temperature and tide lines.

Once in the starting area check the wind so that a game plan for the race can be established. If you prefer sailing alone it's important to use your compass and sail upwind noting the highest and lowest position that you read on each tack. In other words, check the headers and lifts. Also note a median wind range (some point which the wind seems to revolve around as you're sailing on each tack). If you prefer sailing with another boat, which is usually better in the long run, get together with this other boat and split tacks, sailing upwind in opposite directions for a specified period of time. That time may be three or five minutes depending on how long you have before the start. After you've sailed for that time you should both tack and see who's ahead. This knowledge should be taken into account, then sail downwind and do it again, maybe even a couple of more times, alternating who goes to each side of the course. If one side pays off every time, it's probably smart to think about going *toward* that side of the course after the start. If it's an even split or it's close enough that you can't really decide for sure that one side is favored, you probably have an oscillating breeze and should just be sure you're sailing in the lift immediately after the start. Again, a compass is extremely important for determining whether or not you are in a lift or header as you are sailing around the course. The

numbers from your compass should be written down or committed to memory so immediately after the start you will be able to determine whether to tack or continue.

When formulating a pre-race game plan, it's important to remember that even if one side is very favored, that side should be approached with a bit of caution. Plan to play the shifts on the way to the favored side and stay inside of your competition, leaving you able to get back across the course should the wind not go the way you had planned. The less positive you are about which side is favored, the more conservative you should be.

THE START

Figuring out where you're going to start on the line is just as important as deciding which way to go on the beat. The windward leg should be planned before the starting line is ever set as the race committee usually leaves setting the line until the last possible moment.

Once the line is set, checks from both ends should be made. Sight from one end of the line straight through both ends of the line to see if they line up with something on shore nearby. If you can get this line sighting with a marker on the shore or something stationary in the distance, you can tell exactly when you are on the line. You will be able to get a much better, more accurate start time after time, without having the guesswork and anxiety of approaching the line with no definite means of knowing when you are on it.

Once you've gotten a line sight, a check should be made to determine which end of the line is the most favored. In Lasers, it's quite easy to do this even with no one else present and without a compass, should you care not to use one. Reach down the line directly from one end toward the other. Trim your sail so it's just luffing, then cleat it. Once you have the sail trimmed in this manner, tack the boat and head directly toward the other end of the line. If the sail luffs more going the new way, you want to start toward that end of the line. If it luffed more on your original tack, you want to start on the end that you were going toward on that tack. A check similar to this should be made at least three or four times during the ten-minute sequence of your start. If one end is heavily favored, a bit of advantage can be gained by starting near that end.

Below: taking a line sight (transit) is an important step to getting a good start. Here a bush on the shore lines up perfectly with the starting line.

Starting exactly at either end of the starting line is not advantageous as the percentages will be against you for getting a good start. Go for the more consistent, clear air start near the favored end but not immediately *at* the favored end. You'll have a better chance of a good start and be ahead in the long run.

If neither end is particularly favored, a start should be made at the end of the line near where you'd like to go after the start. For instance, if you'd like to tack to port right away, it would be best to start near the starboard end of the line. If you'd like to continue to the left of the course, you will probably have clearer air and get there sooner by starting near the port end of the line. But if there's no end that's particularly favored it's most important to start with clear air and room to leeward for achieving good boat speed. Use the line sight and be right on the line with full upwind speed at the gun.

In the above pictures (taken from in front of the line) the pin end is favored. A group forms at the end of the line (the pin is behind no. 10). By starting *near* but not *at* the favored end the author in 91147 gets the best and safest start.

19

Before the start the author on port tack (in 91147)
approaches a group of starboard tackers.

. . . finishing my tack seconds before the starting
gun with speed and maneuverability that the other
boats lack.

Starting technique

The last couple of minutes before a start should be spent check-
ing your daggerboard and rudder for weeds, making sure everything is trimmed properly for upwind (the cunningham, the
outhaul and the boom vang all set correctly) and then getting
yourself near the end that you want to start from. I prefer
staying on port tack as long as I can to maintain my maneuverability as I approach the starting line. Starboard tack makes it
much more difficult to sail up to the line from behind other
boats. On port tack this can be accomplished quite easily even
up to the last 15 or 20 seconds before the start. By staying on

I sail behind a small group of the starboard tackers.

Finding a hole, I tack into the windward side of the hole . . .

Three to five seconds before the gun my boat is fully accelerated while those around me are trying to regain steerage and accelerate.

At the gun the space to leeward has been used up for acceleration and the hole on the line has been used to its full potential for a good start.

port tack, one is able to watch others on the line establishing their starting positions. With others set on the line it's easier to find a hole and tack into it with forward momentum *and* maneuverability just before it's time to sheet in and accelerate at the start.

The more crowded the starting line the earlier you'll have to put yourself on starboard tack. The less crowded or more spaced out the boats are on the line, the later you can approach the line on port tack, find a hole and tack into it for your start.

The three crucial things to remember in any start are to be sure you're exactly *on* the starting line *on* time and not behind anyone; to make sure that you have some room just to leeward of you to reach off and accelerate just before the starting gun goes, giving you top boat speed at the gun; and to be sure that you have clear air just after the start. These can all be accomplished by approaching the line on port tack, coming up behind the other boats and tacking into the windward side of a hole. The later you do this the less chance there will be of someone coming in to leeward of you and doing the same thing. Also the later that you do this the more defined the line will be in terms of where the crowded parts are and where the holes are. The later you come in to the starting line, the more boat speed you'll have relative to the boats that are trying to hold their position on the line. Using this boat speed when you tack to starboard, you can slowly luff the boats to windward of you, ensuring that they will be significantly slowed and will not be able to drive over you after the gun. Obviously, though, perfect timing is crucial!

Acceleration off the line

A couple of ways to help you accelerate off the starting line are important to know. One is obvious — being able to hit the line with full speed at the gun. This will allow you to jump out ahead of the boats around you which were waiting too close to the line and were unable to accelerate properly for the start. Another way to get yourself off the starting line quickly and away from the other boats, provided you can hold the boat down very flat, is to let your cunningham go completely, making your leech tighter and giving your sail a little more power for the jump off the line. Easing your cunningham should help you to point but will also require harder hiking to keep the boat flat. It's very important that the boat stays flat; if you can't hold the boat down at the start, keep your cunningham very, very tight.

When you're starting you must be sure that you're not pinching. Drive the boat a little bit harder than you would on the open course. Sail it half a degree lower than normal. This will ensure that you're making best use of your foils, helping you to lift to windward, and that you keep your boat speed up — just when you need every bit of speed you can get to pull away from the crowd. Pinching will give you the feeling that you're pointing higher than the other boats when you're actually sliding sideways and eventually will fall into bad air from the boats ahead and to leeward.

Once you have started the boat, use the knowledge you gained just previous to the start to determine which tack to be on. By looking at your compass you can quickly determine whether you're lifted or headed according to the readings you made before the start of the race. If you're headed significantly, try to tack away as soon as possible, even if it means ducking transoms to get on the lift. In the long run, this is more advantageous than staying on the header. If there's one side of the course that you particularly want to sail towards, get that way as soon as you can. If possible, do so by sailing on a lift of some kind.

The gate start

Making a gate start needs a different technique from the normal line start, but much of the same preparation goes into achieving a good gate start. Before the start work out what the wind is doing and which side of the course you'd like to head toward, but because the starting line will be moving, no line sights or references on the line are made.

The gate start puts a lot more emphasis on knowing where you're going just after the start. It makes it vital to know whether the rabbit (pathfinder) is headed or lifted as he sails upwind. You must also consider the speed of the rabbit. If the rabbit is fast, you can safely start in any part of the line and should only think about starting in a lift and whether to start near the beginning or end of the gate sequence. If the rabbit is slow, it's more advantageous to start early in the starting sequence; but try to start on a lift, so when you are headed you can tack and immediately be ahead of the boats that are still starting.

Let's consider a gate start where the rabbit's speed is comparable to the top people in the group. Your major considerations should be whether to start early or late (go left or right) and how to start on a lift. If you want to go left you need to start early. If you want to go right, you want to start late. Starting on a lift means sailing on port tack to leeward and ahead of the gate launch and rabbit until you begin to feel a header on port tack. As you get headed on port you should tack in a space where relatively few boats are nearby and close reach back to the gate launch. If there are boats to leeward, you should wait until there is enough space to gather speed by reaching toward the line and then make your approach. When you round the transom of the gate launch, the boat should be on the fastest possible reach you can attain and it should be

Boat no. 16 makes a perfect gate start.

immediately headed up to close hauled as you cross behind the gate launch. Sometimes, if this is done properly and if there is just the right amount of wind, the reaching can propel you across the transom of the gate launch so quickly that you're able to get on the windward wake of the launch and actually surf upwind, immediately putting you ahead of the boats around you. Should there be a problem with too many boats to leeward of you keeping you from gaining speed and approaching the line quickly, tack back onto port and cross behind the boats that are waiting to start. Remember that on port tack you retain your maneuverability and boat speed much more easily than if you're on starboard tack.

From there the gate start is just like any other start. You are even with a lot of boats around you and have to work very hard to accelerate off the line faster than these other boats. Easing your cunningham when you're able to hike the boat flat can help you to shoot out away from the starting line in moderate breezes. Pulling the cunningham very tight when the breeze is slightly overpowering will help you to retain good boat speed when it's hard to keep the boat flat.

Be sure to keep in mind that the worst thing you can do on any start is to pinch which will eventually cause the boat to go sideways, losing distance on the boats around you.

THE FIRST HUNDRED YARDS

Once on the course and away from the starting line you should begin using the information that you gathered before the start to make tactical decisions to sail the beat properly. If you're headed, especially if you're headed significantly, tack, even if it means bearing off and slowing down to allow yourself room to duck behind a couple of starboard tack boats. If you're headed and you know (from research) it's going to shift back the other way eventually, tack, sail to the next header and tack back. You'll be ahead of the boats that you crossed behind since they were sailing the wrong way.

When you have a good start this is fairly easy to do but often when there's a problem with the start, you're in the second row or pinned in some bad air from a couple of boats that had just a little better start than you did. You have to know how to escape. Remember that clear air is all-important in two-thirds of the sailing that we do. When it's really windy, clear air becomes slightly less important and shifts are the vital thing to concentrate on along with boat speed. But when it's light — especially when it's light — and when it's moderate, clear air is essential, even if it means sailing the wrong way a little while to get it. You can pass a group of boats by sailing on a small header in clear air and getting away from the fleet and then tacking back, whereas you would still be sailing behind them if you kept going the "correct" way.

Getting clear air can mean you'll have an advantage in boat speed over the boats who are staying in a group right after the start. They'll all be slowing themselves down while you're going faster, making up for the distance you're losing by sailing on a header. Obviously if you can get clear air *and* stay on a lift, that's fantastic.

One thing to remember after most starts is that the majority of the boats will be on starboard tack. This means that if you're on starboard tack and behind a couple of boats in bad air you're going to have a hard time breaking through into clear wind.

25

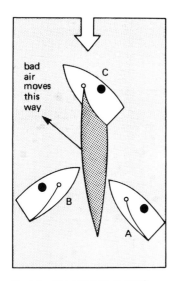

bad air moves this way

C

B

A

Boat A will be in bad air much longer than boat B even if A is moving faster than C. So if things go wrong at the start, port tack may bring clear air sooner.

But if you're on port tack just after the start, it's very easy to break through each starboard tacker's small area of bad wind and find yourself a hole between the starboard tackers where you can either tack back left or get through and go to the right.

The technique that works best for me after a bad start is immediately to get on port tack in the clearest place I can and work my way through the starboard tackers to clear air on the right. The more boats that are ahead of you the more important it is to be on port, if everyone else is on starboard.

Once an area of clear air is found, begin thinking about shifts. If you're lifted, stay on that tack unless you feel it's going to be a persistent lift, in which case tack back left and get on the inside of the lift. But if you're in an oscillating breeze and you're on a lift, stay there. If you're on a header, tack away as soon as you have clear air.

Evaluating priorities

The first hundred yards are so vital and you have to think so quickly that I've devised a system to help me evaluate priorities. The relative importance of clear air, being on the correct tack, the ability to tack easily, good boat speed and the ability to continue on the correct tack are summed up in the chart below. To understand fully how to use the chart, let's examine each of the strategic areas, as they sum up much of what we've been discussing.

Clear air. In light winds, clear air is always ranked most important. Unlike when sailing in most other winds, when it's light, it's imperative to have clear air so that you can develop even average boat speed. If your speed is less than average, because you are eating bad air behind a couple of other boats, you'll be quickly left behind, no matter how well you play the other options.

In medium to heavy winds, clear air becomes slightly less important since speed is not affected by dirty wind as much as in light conditions. Clear air is least important when the breeze is very shifty and strong, for then where you go becomes almost as important as how fast you go.

Correct tack. As the wind builds to over five knots, sailing on the correct tack becomes the top priority. It takes over from clear air since, as the wind increases, average boat speed can be achieved even if the air is somewhat obstructed. So, as you

Strategy	Wind direction and speed											
	Oscillating less than 10 degrees			Oscillating more than 10 degrees			Persistently shifting less than 10 degrees**			Persistently shifting more than 10 degrees**		
	0 – 5 knots	5 – 15 knots	15+ knots	0 – 5 knots	5 – 15 knots	15+ knots	0 – 5 knots	5 – 15 knots	15+ knots	0 – 5 knots	5 – 15 knots	15+ knots
Clear air	1	2	3	1	4	4	1	2	3	1	2	3
Correct tack	2	1	1	2	1	1	3	1	1	2	1	1
Ability to tack easily	5	5	5	4	3	3	5	5	5	5	5	5
Good boat speed *	4	3	2	5	5	5	2	3	2	3	3	2
Continue on correct tack	3	4	4	3	2	2	4	4	4	4	4	4

Key: 1 = most important, 5 = least important
* assumes near-average boat speed relative to the fleet when not fully concentrating on boat speed
** measured in the number of degrees the wind will shift over one windward leg

come off the line in a fair breeze, going the correct way should be the main priority, as it allows you to gain more (or lose less) than any of the other considerations.

Notice that in light winds, sailing on the correct tack is still very important, although less so than in the higher wind ranges. Only when the wind is light and shifting persistently less than 10 degrees does correct tack take a back seat to anything other than clear air.

Ability to tack easily. This category has a surprisingly low ranking on the priority chart. When I realized I'd rated this area so poorly in nearly every wind condition, it occurred to me that this was one of the largest problems I'd been experiencing on the race course. Perhaps it's been a problem for you too.

How many times have you started next to a group of boats and been really frustrated because you were sailing into a header, but just "couldn't" tack because of all the boats on your windward quarter and your strong reluctance to tack and take a few transoms? You wait and wait, and finally they begin tacking off. But by the time you're able to tack, the shift has gone back the other way. Or in a persistent shift, by the time you are able to tack, so many people have gone to the correct side that you end up miles behind and have to struggle the rest of the race just to catch up.

From the heavy emphasis placed on correct tack, it appears that you should almost always tack when it appears advantageous to do so, even if it means taking transoms and losing a little distance in the short run. After all, the more important priority is going the right way. Only in a very shifty breeze is it recommended that you place emphasis on positioning yourself where you can tack at will. Even then, getting on the correct tack should be weighed more heavily in the decision-making process.

Good boat speed. Boat speed plays an important part in any race and should always be considered important to doing well. However, in the table, notice that in very shifty winds boat speed takes a back seat to all other factors — correct tack, clear air, ability to tack easily and continue on the correct tack. This is because when the shifts are relatively large, position (largely the result of the other four factors) yields much higher dividends and should therefore be the first priority.

But when the breeze is steady, boat speed becomes a much more important factor because less distance is gained per shift. In other words, if it's shifty, think mostly about the shifts; if it's steady, think about boat speed.

Continue on correct tack. This is a very important area that is often overlooked. It deals with situations such as letting a port tacker cross in front of you rather than forcing him to tack on your lee bow, possibly forcing you the wrong way. There are many times early in the beat when similar close situations arise and a fast decision must be made about what to do, whether you are the right-of-way boat or not. Using the chart makes decision-making easier. For instance, in shifty winds, it is advantageous to stay on the proper tack as long as the shift lasts. If you're on the correct tack, most of the time it's better to duck a close port tacker than to have them tack on your lee bow and hurt you. But if you're not on the best tack, call for rights and force your competitor to tack the wrong way, and then tack away yourself, onto the correct tack.

On the other hand, if you're on port tack and going the right way, you would probably do best to go out of your way to duck a starboard tacker rather than be forced off in the wrong direction. In a steady breeze, though, this is not so much the case. Suffice it to say, that whenever you're going the way you want to go, try to keep other boats from forcing you to do otherwise.

THE BEAT

As you're sailing up the beat, work with your compass. Make sure you watch what it's doing. It will tell you headers and lifts if you look at it and remember the numbers. Sail the boat fast, occasionally glancing at the compass. Trust it. It *does* work. Watch the other boats on the course, watch people who are going to the opposite side of the course from you and learn from them but don't let them create *your* game plan. Stick to what you've decided is the best way to go because of wind or current. If there are a lot of boats on the left side of the course that look like they're in a big lift on port tack, that doesn't necessarily mean you have to get over there right away. If you are also on port tack and you're on a lift, stay on the lift. Chances are you'll be headed, tack and then be much closer to or even ahead of them. Hold out — don't panic. Too many people see another boat getting ahead of them and run over that way just in time to get headed again coming back the other way. Chasing shifts, as I call it, is the downfall of many a very fast sailor. They see someone on a better angle and sail that way; by the time they get there that breeze is gone. And so are the people that they were with before.

Using your compass properly also means finding out before the start how big the shifts are going to be. Then when you're

The author sailing upwind in 18 to 20 knots. Note the tensioning of the cunningham. The body is thrown aft as the bow goes into the waves and moves back forward as the bow lifts again. Note also that the mainsheet has been eased to keep the boat from heeling over and stalling.

How flat you should hold the boat varies in different breezes. For medium air and relatively smooth water (*above and opposite*) the boat should maintain a slight heel which keeps it powerful — this amount of heel is usually referred to as "keeping the boat flat". *Right:* in heavy air and more waves a little more heel is acceptable. This shows the amount of heel that is fast in 15 knots and above.

on the race course sailing upwind, you know if you still have another five degrees to be headed before you need tack. Or you know that if you're just a couple of degrees above what should be median, then you should probably stay on that tack for a while. Having that range established before you start is extremely important to being able to sail the windward leg properly. When you're on a lift and in clear air sailing upwind, concentrate on your boat speed, work the boat through the waves, sail it fast. As you get the boat going really well, take a few seconds to glance around and notice what's happening on the rest of the course, then come back to your boat speed. In light air this means staying as still as you can in the boat, sitting up by the daggerboard well and heeling the boat just a little bit to leeward. In medium air this means sitting just in the front of the cockpit and working the boat with your body through the waves. When it heels over, hike it down; before it becomes too flat, sit in a little bit and bear off; when waves get large or when a big set of waves is coming, ease the sheet and bear off a little bit for good

driving speed. Keep the boat just heeled slightly to leeward most of the time: five degrees is approximately correct.

Sail controls

When it gets really windy a lot of boom vang is required to enable you to ease the mainsheet without having the boom go very far up in the air. The boom will travel outboard away from the boat as if it were on an extended traveler. As you're overpowered, more and more mainsheet should be eased out and the boat should be steered slightly more away from the wind. Use the mainsheet to control the heel of the boat. When you become too flat, sheet in; when the boat heels over too much and starts to pound on waves, ease the mainsheet out — flattening the boat — and bear off.

The cunningham has two positions on my boat. It's either all the way on or all the way off. It's all the way off whenever the wind is such that I can hold the boat down with no problem. When I'm having to hike relatively hard, the cunningham goes all the way on, which means that the sail, in most cases, is touching the boom.

It is essential to be able to adjust the boom vang while sailing. *Left:* to put the vang on, I head the boat into the wind and use my forward hand to grab the boom vang line where it leaves the cleat. Note the mainsheet is still in this hand. *Right:* now I move my aft hand, still holding the tiller, to the boom next to the block. Using both hands and all my body weight I push down on the boom and tighten the vang.

Steering

In addition to these techniques, good boat speed upwind demands intelligent steering and hiking. In light air as little tiller motion and body movement as possible should be used. As the breeze picks up and you're starting to sit out over the side a little bit, your body can be used to help the boat to turn. By hiking down hard to windward you can help yourself steer the boat away from the wind. By sitting up temporarily you allow the boat to heel and help it to head up into the wind. Note that you're not turning the boat with your body, but helping the boat turn by altering the underwater shape.

Ducking other boats

Another point that's important to mention for sailing upwind is that when ducking other boats on the windward leg (for instance, a port tack boat crossing behind a starboard tack boat or a starboard tack boat that's allowing the port tacker to cross ahead) it's very important to ease the mainsheet as you bear off. In light and medium air easing the mainsheet allows you to hold your speed at a higher level than keeping it overtrimmed. In heavy air if you don't ease the mainsheet you won't be able to bear off far enough and will probably end up hitting the boat that you were going to duck behind. Even if hitting the other boat is not a problem, by trying to bear off without easing the mainsheet your boat will heel too much and stall, causing it to slow down, leaving you farther to leeward than if you had eased your mainsheet and maintained a flat boat.

Wave technique

Dealing with waves upwind requires a lot of body movement. As the bow is lifted by a wave your body should be in a position that is just beginning to weight the boat by pushing down on it. In other words, as the bow lifts you should have just bounced up in the air a little bit and as the boat reaches the top of the wave your body should be putting full downward momentum pressure on the boat, trying to keep the bow in the water. It's very important not to let the bow of the boat come out of the water allowing it to fall back down and slam into the next wave. Use your body and the momentum that you can achieve by weighting and unweighting the boat to try to hold the bow in the water. Also use the mainsheet and tiller as you're sailing over these waves. As you reach the top of the wave, or come to

While sailing to windward the outhaul can be tensioned by grasping the outhaul line with each hand on either side of the cleat. Hold the boom with your forward hand, pull the outhaul in with your aft hand, and take up the slack through the cleat with your forward hand. The boat will heel slightly to leeward during this maneuver so practice it to avoid tragedies — especially in heavy air. It's important to keep hold of both the sheet and tiller during the entire sequence.

Wave technique: *Left:* as the boat bears away over the crest of the wave the mainsheet is eased and the body thrown forward.

Right: as the bow punches into a new wave the mainsheet is pulled in and the body rolled back (see also diagram below).

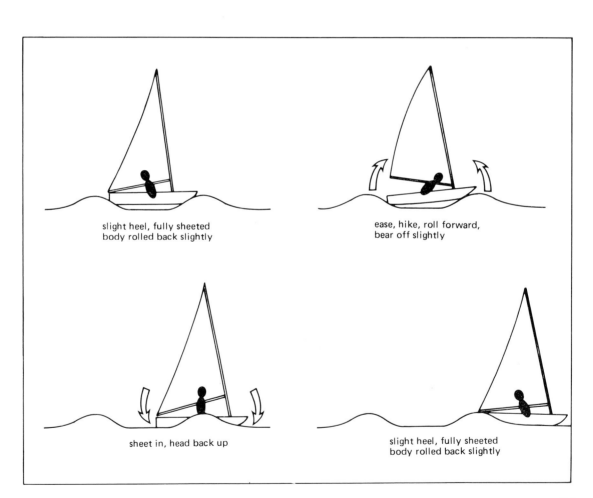

slight heel, fully sheeted
body rolled back slightly

ease, hike, roll forward,
bear off slightly

sheet in, head back up

slight heel, fully sheeted
body rolled back slightly

a set of short waves, the mainsheet should be eased. Hike very hard and steer the boat away from the wind, keeping the bow on the wave while moving down its back side. As you come to the next wave or set of short waves, sheet in, head up, unweight the boat a little bit and let it heel to leeward. Then repeat the process as the bow is lifted by the wave, hiking hard, easing the mainsheet and bearing off down the back of the wave.

Obviously this process cannot be used for every wave on the course, and it's not necessary for every wave. It is necessary, however, to use this process to keep the boat moving through the larger sets of waves. Remember to keep the boat moving forward. If the boat is heeled over, if it slams on a wave or if it stalls temporarily by hitting a wave too squarely, it's going to stop and go sideways and you'll lose distance to windward. By easing the mainsheet and bearing off slightly before you get to a set of short waves, your power is increased, helping you punch through the waves and losing less distance to windward in the long run.

The only time in a Laser that you don't sit right at the front of the cockpit for upwind is when you're sailing directly into a chop — in other words when you're sailing at right angles to the waves and it's very windy. Then you have to move back approximately one butt-width or 14 inches allowing the bow to stay high enough in the air that it won't submerge itself in the

In a strong gust ease the mainsheet quite substantially. This is a very powerful arrangement and keeps the boat moving. It's important when sailing this way to have the boom vang very tight so when the main is eased the boom moves out horizontally, not rising in the air.

I can't stress enough the importance of easing the mainsheet in
very heavy winds, otherwise the
boat will simply lean over and
pound in the waves. *Left:* here I
am approaching a wave that looks
as though it will break . . .

. . . by easing the mainsheet and
letting the sail luff slightly some
of the power is lost. Note that
the boat is not heeled too much.

When you're through the wave, re-
sheet the main and head the boat
up. Remember to use your upper
body — extending in a puff or
wave and straightening up in
lighter spots.

waves that are approaching. Now it should be cautioned that as
you sail the windward leg of any course, one or two or even
three or four waves over the bow is normal. If you never get a
wave over the bow when it's windy, you're sitting too far aft
in your boat. The occasional wave may come over your bow but
most of them will go just underneath with no problem. That's
the guide to where you should be sitting as you're racing
upwind.

If you're beating with the waves coming at you sideways again
you can move back to the front of the cockpit so that your
forward leg is approximately three to four inches back from the
position of the ratchet block.

Below: to let the vang off while
approaching the weather mark, I
put the mainsheet in my tiller
hand, freeing my forward hand to
pop the vang off slightly just
before rounding.

Approaching the windward mark

As you sail up the beat continue playing the shifts using your
compass and working towards the side of the course that you
feel is favored. As you get half-way or two-thirds of the way to
the weather mark, two groups of boats should be apparent: one
on the right and one on the left of the course. If one side is
becoming obviously favored you should try to work toward that
side, staying inside and ahead of any groups that are coming
across. Stay away from the lay lines. Lay lines should not be
approached until approximately the last tenth of the windward
leg. Getting on a lay line too early means that if you're headed,
boats ahead and to leeward of you can tack and be further
ahead or pass you when they never could before. If you're on
the lay line and get lifted, you're overlaying the mark, wasting
distance that someone else is taking advantage of.

When you do get near the weather mark there are a lot of approaches to consider. If you're relatively well up in the fleet you can play shifts right up to the windward mark and round it with no problem, but as you get farther down the fleet and more boats are rounding the mark just in front of you, a different game plan must be established.

Especially in light and medium air large groups of boats that are approaching the windward mark on the lay line are leaving tremendous holes in the wind to leeward of them. A position that allows these boats to take any of your wind is extremely bad for approaching the windward mark. When there are big groups an attempt should be made to stay to leeward and ahead of them, or to cross through or behind them and tack outside in clearer air enabling you to round the windward mark freely. Try to tack just past the lay line to avoid boats tacking in your wind and forcing you to tack again. So either stay inside and to leeward of a group, especially when approaching on port, or, in the case of a starboard tack approach, cross and go outside of the group leaving you clear air and freedom of mobility when approaching the windward mark.

Rounding the windward mark.

At the beginning of a roll tack the boat should be heeled to leeward slightly to help it steer into the wind.

As the boat begins to head up into the wind the main should be sheeted in hard and the tiller pushed over to its maximum turning point.

TACKING

To get around the course as quickly as possible good roll tacks must be utilized. A good roll tack goes something like this: you unweight the boat slightly by leaning in or sitting up temporarily. This allows the boat to heel slightly to leeward, and as it heels it will try to head itself up into the wind. Allow it to do so by releasing the pressure on the tiller extension, letting the rudder follow the boat. As the sail begins to luff, sheet in all the way, hike the boat down hard to windward and push the tiller as far as necessary to turn the boat onto the new tack. As the sail comes across you should pull your body in with your legs and duck underneath the boom, while at the same time easing approximately an arm's length of mainsheet out and straightening the tiller. Push yourself onto the new side, setting the tiller extension down on the deck (angled forward so it won't fall backwards into the boat). With your old tiller hand grab the mainsheet and with your new tiller hand grab the tiller extension. If the boat is heeling over too much, ease the mainsheet as you get hiking to flatten the boat down. If the boat is not heeling enough to leeward, trim the mainsheet slightly and slowly bear off at the same time leaning in to help the boat heel.

As the sail begins to luff a sharp hike to windward will help to spin the boat and keep the sail filled longer.

By remaining on the windward side until the sail begins to come across the skipper leaves the boat in a heeled position for the new tack.

As the sail comes across the mainsheet should be eased and the body moved toward the windward side, the tiller extension should be pushed through in front of the body and as on every tack and gybe the skipper should face forward to keep in touch with the surrounding conditions.

As the boat finishes its tack and the sail fills, it is heeling to leeward slightly. The tiller should be kept in the center of the boat behind the skipper's back as he flattens the boat down. After the boat is back on course and flat the skipper can drop the tiller extension and change hands quickly before the boat begins to head up.

Roll tacking in heavier air. First the boat is allowed to heel slightly to leeward.

As the sail luffs the boat is heeled to weather and the main is sheeted in.

As the sail comes across the sheet is released so the boom pops up and over the skipper's head. Note the tiller extension is out in front of the body; the tiller is turned to its full turning extent and the mainsheet is still in the forward hand.

The skipper moves across to the new side as the boat finishes its turn. As the boat is moving on its way again the skipper drops the tiller extension from behind his back and grabs the mainsheet out of his new back hand. Finally the new back hand grabs the tiller extension.

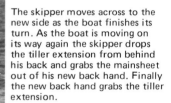

Roll tacks are crucial to taking advantage of windshifts and tight situations around the windward leg, and every Laser sailor must know how to roll tack his boat properly. The windier it gets the less you need to heel the boat to the new leeward side and the quicker you have to go across. Also in heavy wind you can sometimes use the waves to help you turn the boat. Turning the boat into the wind just as a wave is going to hit the bow will help it turn the rest of the way around.

Most important to the success of a roll tack after you've crossed through the eye of the wind is to have the mainsheet *in* your hand and be ready to ease it immediately if the boat is heeling too far to leeward. Most unsuccessful roll tacks are caused by the boat heeling too much to leeward on the new tack, forcing the skipper to hike very hard and causing the boat to stall because it's heeled so far. Simply ease the mainsheet to avoid this problem.

For reaching, ease the boom vang slightly so the upper leech of the sail takes on a shape like this (*below*). The twist is especially effective for heavy air reaching since it lets air spill out. Also, a tight vang would bring the boom close to the waves — if the boom hits the water the boat is likely to capsize.

THE REACH

As you round the windward mark there's a sequence of things that should happen. In light and medium air just before you get to the windward mark you should ease your outhaul slightly. In all winds just as you approach the weather mark the vang should be eased slightly from its upwind position. Upwind you're always sailing with the vang just a little bit tighter than the point where the boom's sheeted to. In other words, as you race upwind the vang should never be slack but just as you get to the windward mark you should sheet the sail in all the way to two-blocked and pop the vang off so it's just slack when the sail is two-blocked. This gives the boat more power by straightening the mast for light and medium air reaches. It also allows the sail to twist and lifts the boom up higher in the air for heavy winds. This makes it easier to sail heavy air reaches, without the problem of the boom dragging in the water, trying to tip you over.

As you round the windward mark the sail should immediately go out to its proper position for the reach. It's helpful to have telltales on your sail about 14 inches back from the luff and as low on the sail as is possible while still keeping them away from seams that they might catch on. Use these tell-tales on the

It's faster and more efficient to trim the main directly from the boom block on reaches and runs.

reaches to determine whether or not your sail is trimmed properly. Most people sail on a reach with their sails overtrimmed. The use of telltales can prevent this problem.

Once your sail is in the proper position for reaching, the cunningham comes off completely and whenever possible the board should be lifted to approximately halfway up. When it's really windy it's more important to continue planing than it is to reduce drag by lifting the board. So lift the board whenever you get the chance! In very high winds it's often a help to lift the board before rounding the mark.

As you're sailing the reach, sheet the sail right from the boom, never cleating the mainsheet and constantly watching the telltales to help you adjust the sail properly.

High or low course?

As you round the windward mark a decision should be made as to whether you're going to sail high or low on the reach. Several factors play a part in this decision. If you're just ahead of a group it's probably more advantageous to sail high, keeping them from encroaching on your wind and causing you to go slow. If you're just behind a group you can probably make out by sailing low, shortening the distance between the two marks while the other boats play luffing games.

Another factor to think about on the reach is changing windstrength. If you're sailing in a dying breeze, you want to sail low leaving you in a position to sail closer to the wind in the lighter air for better speed at the end of the leg. If the breeze is increasing you can probably sail higher, maintaining a better speed throughout the entire leg as the breeze will be stronger when you're bearing off and sailing a lower course at the end of the leg. If it's puffy and/or shifty you want to sail low in the header and/or puffs and sail higher in the light spots and/or lifts.

All these factors have to be considered simultaneously. For instance: if you're at the weather mark in a header and a puff and the wind is going to be dying but there's a group of boats right behind you, you have to decide whether you can get far enough away from them by sailing down on the puff and up later in the lull or if you need to stay high with them to protect your position in clear air. It becomes rather complicated but understanding and *using* the methods of sailing a good reach can make it much easier to do well.

By angling the legs back the loose hiking strap that is necessary for upwind sailing becomes tighter and helps to keep the body out of the water on reaches. Angling the upper body forward or back will help to lift the bow or depress it, depending on your situation with waves.

On planing reaches weight should be kept aft to keep the bow out of the water and prevent it from digging through the waves. Here, already planing, the author gets a large puff and begins to ease the mainsheet and hike out and aft to keep the bow up and the boat flat.

In another puff the boat is made to bear off, the bow is kept out of the water by hiking back and the heel of the boat is controlled by trimming or easing the sail and hiking out.

Still in a puff of 20 to 25 knots the boat sails into a wave. At this point it must be headed up and the sail trimmed in to keep moving fast. Hiking more aft will also help keep the bow out of the water.

Trim

In light and medium air on a reach good speed is achieved by constantly watching the trim of your sail. Use the telltales to maintain proper trim, sit forward in the boat, near the daggerboard well; and in very light air keep the boat heeled slightly to leeward. In medium winds the boat can be heeled just a bit to leeward or perfectly flat but never let the boat heel to windward for any length of time.

Wave technique

As it get windier with surfing and planing conditions, sailing the reach fast becomes a matter of trimming the sail, using your body to help the boat turn, steering for each wave and anticipating where the boat will be two waves later. Keep your boat sailing downhill; keep it going down the waves.

One of the things that hurts a boat's speed more than anything is not being able to steer the boat down a wave properly because the sail is overtrimmed or is not being eased fast enough. When you are hit with a puff in a Laser, the boat will instantly heel to leeward. The same thing happens when a wave is lifting your transom from behind. Most people try to hike the boat down rather than easing the sail to maintain the boat's flatness. It's really fast, however, to use the sail to keep the boat flat. When a wave lifts your transom or when a puff hits you, ease the sail

Popping out of the wave, I head the boat more downwind again to continue surfing or planing.

Once the boat is flattened out and surfing down a wave, the legs are used to pull the upper body straight and the heel of the boat is controlled again by sail trim. This picture also shows the correct daggerboard position for the reach.

immediately, then hike out. Then trim the sail back in, pumping one or two times to help the boat get on the wave. Once you're sailing on a wave or once you're planing, slide back in the boat about a foot from where you were. This helps the bow stay out of the water. Trim the sail properly for the wind. If you head up the sail has to come in, if you need to bear off the sail has to go out. Keep the boat going down the wave or on the plane as long as possible. If you start to slow on a wave or if you start to fall off a plane, head the boat up, sheet in and move forward slightly all at the same time to keep the boat moving fast.

When it's windy sit back just far enough to keep the bow from plowing into waves. Sit forward in the light spots and when you get the boat going down a wave or on a plane, ease back. Play the mainsheet constantly and use the tiller as little as possible. Use your body and the mainsheet to help turn the boat and keep it going downhill.

One final reminder on easing the vang for heavy weather reaches. If you're light or if you're heavy, it's crucial to ease the boom vang just before you get to the windward mark. Light-weights need this to allow the sail to twist and keep the boom out of the water in puffy and windy conditions. Heavyweights need the power of having the sail full because the mast is straighter. It works for everybody to ease the boom vang off for downwind.

Just before performing a reach-to-reach gybe the author glances upwind to check for puffs.

As I begin the gybe the boat is heeled slightly to weather, steered downwind and the main eased out a little.

The boat is turned more rapidly as it slows.

The reach-to-reach gybe is perhaps the most difficult maneuver in the Laser in terms of timing and coordination. The sequence above shows the technique for medium winds.

GYBING

The gybe mark of a Laser course poses some interesting problems. Not only do we have to perform the difficult maneuver of gybing the boat in close proximity to the mark and to other boats, but we also have to try for the inside rounding position as well as deciding whether to sail high or low on the next reach. You need to give this rounding a lot of consideration well before reaching the mark.

My major concern at any gybe mark, especially one that is going to have a tight reach for the next leg, is to round inside of any other boats in the area. If I do get stuck outside for some reason, I try my best to set myself up in a position where I can immediately gain control of the boat inside of me just after the gybe. This usually means rounding a bit wider than the other boat (to get behind him) and immediately sailing high on the next leg.

Occasionally the second reach will be very broad. If this is the case, and if you're in a large group of boats, it may be advantageous to continue slightly past the mark on a downwind course and gybe later — or sail low immediately after the gybe mark. In this situation rounding inside is not so important. But on most reaches you should strive for an inside position at the gybe mark.

Light and medium air gybes

The gybe can be a relatively quick and easy maneuver if you've done it enough times and understand when and how to turn the

46

As the wind comes around to the new side of the sail I duck under the boom, straighten the tiller, flatten the boat and give a sharp tug on the mainsheet.

As the sail fills on the new side the boat is steered more downwind temporarily to keep it under control and is flattened by my weight on the new side. Once the

boat is under control and sailing straight I can drop the tiller and change hands.

boat and move your body. The movements of boat and body are relatively the same in all wind conditions. The difference is that the magnitude of turning and rolling of the boat with your body is increased in lighter wind. In light wind as you start turning the boat and beginning the gybe, the forward hand that's on the mainsheet should also grab the hiking strap. The aft hand that's holding the tiller extension should be put in front of the body. The tiller should be turned to an angle approximately 45 degrees off center and the boat should be rolled hard to windward as it is turned. The boat will spin on its daggerboard and will heel very far to windward, keeping the windward rail in the water through the turn. As the sail begins to fall across the boat over to the new side, you should move to the new windward side and flatten the boat *quickly*. This will prevent the mainsheet from catching around the corner of the transom. At the same time the body is being moved the tiller should also be straightened to keep the boat moving on its forward course. At this time your tiller hand is your forward hand and behind your back and your mainsheet hand is your aft hand in front of your chest. Once the boat is flat and moving on its course again your hands can be switched by

Below: a reach-to-reach gybe in lighter wind. The boat is heeled farther to weather which helps the main to come across to the new side. Note the aft hand on the windward rail (for balance), still holding the tiller extension.

Use the tiller extension to help grab the aft purchase of the mainsheet.

Then drop the tiller with the extension swiveled towards the new side.

Throw the main hard towards the new side and keep the body on what will be the new leeward side.

Above: a run-to-run gybe in light air means going from by the lee on one gybe to by the lee on the other, so you're actually heading up as you gybe.

dropping the tiller extension momentarily, grabbing the main-sheet and then picking up the tiller extension with your other hand.

This same process is repeated in all winds with the only difference being that the boat is not heeled as far to windward nor allowed to stay heeled as long in stronger winds. And as the wind gets very heavy, the boat must also be steered back down-wind just after the gybe in something of an "S" turn to keep it under control and moving forward.

An easy way to tell how much the boat should be rolled in the different conditions is that whenever it's very easy to hike the boat down fast after a gybe, in other words in winds under maybe six knots or so, the boom should hit the water as it crosses to the new side. In medium air, say up to 15 knots, the boom should just touch the water or just miss touching the water as it crosses to the new side. And in heavy air it's best to try not to let the boom touch the water so you can avoid the risk of capsizing to leeward after the gybe.

Heavy air gybes

A couple of comments on gybing in heavy air, which is most difficult. A lot of people have problems in heavy air because they don't gybe the boat forcefully enough. They hesitate in the middle of the gybe, waiting for the sail to come across; when it starts to come across they steer the boat back straight downwind, stopping its turning motion. The sail fills once again on the same side and they capsize to leeward. Now they've got two problems: they have to right the boat *and* they still have to gybe.

48

As the sail fills on the new side, stay on that side until the sail is out near its normal position.

As the sail goes out to almost its full out position, take the tiller extension and begin moving slowly toward the new side.

The boom needs pushing the last few inches. Once the boom is out past 90 degrees the boat can be heeled to windward and the sail will stay out on its own.

When it's time to gybe in heavy air, *do it*. Turn the boat relatively hard, make sure the sail is going to come across, maybe even give it a pull and when you *know* it's coming across, go to the other side and hike the boat back down — and don't hesitate. Hesitation causes a lot of problems in a heavy air gybe.

The other time that people have problems is just after the gybe. If you haven't been quick enough to get to the new high side, the boat will be heeling over to leeward, boom dragging, trying to head up into the wind or capsize. Easing the mainsheet out two or three feet right at the time when the sail fills on the new side will help to avoid this problem and allow you a little bit more time to get in position on the windward side. Easing the mainsheet acts as a shock absorber when the sail fills on the new side and lessens the possibility of a capsize to leeward.

Below: in heavy air not so much roll is used to help the boat gybe but other movements are still the same. The important thing in heavy air is to be sure the sail is coming across. This can be done by turning fast and hard through the gybe. When the sail is definitely coming across, the boat may be steered back downwind in an S fashion to counteract the heel to the new leeward side that may cause a capsize. As the sail fills (and is eased slightly) on the new side, the boat should be steered from behind the skipper's back until under control and then he should switch hands. As with any tack or gybe you should face forward throughout the entire maneuver.

THE RUN

Straight downwind sailing is a different matter from reaching and different considerations are important. Of course, when you're on the run you want to try to stay out of the wind-shadows of boats behind you. If there's a large group straight upwind from you, you might move to one side or the other of that group to keep your air clear for speed.

Trim

Trimming the boat properly is very similar to sailing on the reach. You want to keep the bow from digging through the waves but you also want to keep the transom from dragging too much. Lean forward when you're about to surf and lean back as you begin to go fast. Your body weight should be kept *over* your legs for quick mobility and the mainsheet and tiller extension should both be in front of your chest for easy access and movement in any direction.

Straight downwind sailing in very light winds. Note the body position — right next to the daggerboard although the legs are still in the cockpit. The boat is heeled slightly and because my weight is forward the transom is lifting out of the water.

Left: from a different angle note the amount of heel to windward for straight downwind sailing, which decreases the amount of hull that is in the water and neutralizes helm.

Right: if you have trouble keeping the sail full or if the boom swings inboard, let the boom out past 90 degrees to the boat. Then heel the boat to windward to fill the sail and hold the boom out.

Sailing by the lee

I usually find that if I try to sail by the lee downwind I'm able to go relatively quickly compared to the other boats. Sailing by the lee involves having the breeze come across the leech of your sail first rather than the luff. In light wind, sailing by the lee is definitely faster and in heavy wind it's more stable, so it's also faster. I'm assuming, of course, that sailing by the lee is not taking you too far from the mark. You can sail by the lee in light wind by easing the sail way out, a little bit past 90 degrees, heeling the boat to windward so the boom holds itself out and bearing off until the telltales begin flowing toward the mast. Keep the sail in this configuration and keep the air flow going across the sail. As the wind picks up you may sheet in a bit more to keep the boat more stable and keep it from rolling to windward. But still try to keep the flow going from leech to luff by watching the telltales and having them flow toward the mast. If there are waves on the course get on the tack that takes you as close to straight down the waves as you can go while still heading close to the mark. Sail by the lee, pumping (legally!) and heading up whenever you need power to surf down a wave.

The downwind technique of sailing by the lee. Note the direction of the telltale as it flows backwards from leech to luff.

Staying in puffs

Once you're going well downwind, concentrate on staying in puffs, which means looking behind you a lot and getting in front of the puffs. By staying in a puff you can keep your speed up for more of the leg and get down the leg faster and it's worth turning even 20 or 30 degrees off course to get in a good puff. Try to meet it as it comes downwind and get it as it first starts to go by your area, carrying it whichever way it is moving across the course. Use the puffs to your advantage to move up and over people that are in front of you and keep your boat going down waves as fast as possible. At the same time, however, be careful of boats directly upwind of you that may be in your wind.

Death rolling

Straight downwind we're confronted with another problem which is that of death rolling. A little overbalancing, a lift, a big puff, or maybe steering just a little too sharply down a wave can easily capsize us to windward.

To avoid this, it helps to keep your hands in front of your body. When you start to roll to windward trim the mainsheet in while reaching across with your tiller extension in hand and, trying to head the boat up at the same time, grab the leeward rail to pull your body to the leeward side. All these forces should counteract the death roll, if done in time.

There will be occasions though when everyone has the chance to experience a death roll. The most embarrassing, of course, is in light to moderate air when we're really not concentrating on how far the boat is heeling to windward and a small puff gets us, or we lose our balance just a little bit and tip over to windward. In this case it's very easy to right the boat, just climb up over the weather side and get on the daggerboard. Grab the mainsheet and throw the sail down into the water. Then right the boat and sail on as if it were a leeward capsize.

In very heavy air the death roll happens very quickly and the boat instantly begins to turtle. Also the hull is spun to leeward

To counteract the dreaded death roll, use your tiller hand to pull your body to leeward, pull in the mainsheet and head up.

of where the sail or mast hits the water. In this case you've got to jump out of the boat, swim around (or underneath), get up on the daggerboard and right the boat. But the problem here lies in the fact that the mast and sail are to windward of the boat. If you try to jump over the rail and get back in the cockpit as soon as the boat starts to come up, it's going to capsize right away again. The way to right the boat properly after a death roll in very heavy air is to get on the daggerboard and begin righting it; as it comes up wrap your arms and legs around the daggerboard and go underwater with it as the boat rights itself. If the boat tips all the way over again you'll be on top of the daggerboard ready to right it and get on your way. But more times than not the weight of your body on the daggerboard will keep the boat from rolling over again. As the mast gets vertical you can reach underwater to the rail on the new windward side. You can often grab the boat and hold it down so it won't capsize again. Then climb back in and sail on your way again.

The key things to remember, though, in avoiding a death roll are to try and keep the sail trimmed in a little bit more if you're out of control than if you were comfortable. Keep your hands in front of your body and if you do start to roll to windward sheet in, try to head up by pulling the tiller to leeward and grab the rail on the leeward side to pull your body to leeward to counteract the forces of the boat rolling to windward.

Rounding the leeward mark

The leeward mark rounding is one of the toughest roundings on the course in terms of things that must be done in a small amount of time. Just before you round the mark the cunningham should be put onto the proper tension for upwind. The board should be lifted up all the way and then put down all the way to ensure that no weeds have caught themselves around it. Then the mainsheet should be taken back through the ratchet block and the slack taken out of the mainsheet between the block on the boom and the ratchet in the boat.

As you round the mark the mainsheet has to come in while you're turning. A nice smooth rounding needs to be achieved with the boat right next to the mark as it goes by on its upwind course. Sheeting in the sail properly while turning the boat can only be done with both hands trimming the mainsheet (the aft hand still holding the tiller extension and steering). The boat should be heeled slightly to leeward, the sail should be trimmed

Recovery from a capsize to windward caused by a death roll. The technique of using the mainsheet to pull the sail down into the water works beautifully in less than extreme conditions.

Rounding the leeward mark. Just before arriving at the mark push down the daggerboard.

Tighten the cunningham if needed for the beat.

To trim in a lot of sheet in a short time use the hand-over-hand method: hold the tiller extension in one finger and a thumb while the other fingers handle the sheet . . .

in using both hands and the tiller turned slightly to leeward to help the boat head up. As the boat starts to heel more as you reach the upwind sailing position, push out into the upwind hiking position.

At some point after rounding the leeward mark when the water is smooth and boats around you are not threatening the boat should be luffed up straight into the wind for just a second and the boom vang replaced to its proper upwind tension.

To get quickly back onto course after replacing the boom vang tension, grab the boom near the forward boom block and pull it hard to windward. The boat will turn itself away from the wind. When it reaches a point that is near the direction you want to be sailing, release the boom and grab the mainsheet, trim back in and get going on your course once again.

THE FINISH

The finish is a part of the race that many people pay too little attention to. Picking the correct end of the line to finish on is just as important as picking the correct end of the starting line, especially when other boats are in close proximity to you. At

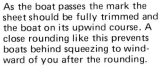

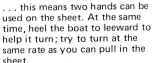

. . . this means two hands can be used on the sheet. At the same time, heel the boat to leeward to help it turn; try to turn at the same rate as you can pull in the sheet.

As the boat passes the mark the sheet should be fully trimmed and the boat on its upwind course. A close rounding like this prevents boats behind squeezing to windward of you after the rounding.

the start you want to start on the end of the line that is closest to the wind. At the finish you want to finish at the end of the line that is farthest away from the wind, or closest to where the leeward mark is. Unlike the start, where you're starting *near* an end, at the finish you should finish right *at* the end. The reason for this is that if it's very close between you and another boat, if you are right at the end you know precisely when to head the boat straight into the wind to cross the line giving yourself possibly an extra half boat length of distance when done properly. Also, if you're on the closest end you sail less distance than the midline finisher.

When the start and finish line are one and the same, as on a split windward leg, it's easy to know which end of the finish line to finish at — the opposite of the one that you wanted to start at. But when a new finish line is laid at the end of a course, a decision must be made where to finish. Remember to pick an end to finish and try to pick the one that appears closest. Normally the committee boat will be the closest end in an upwind finish because the marker is put in the water first, then the committee boat is anchored second, which usually means it will drift downwind a little farther than anticipated, biasing the finish line slightly to its side. Keep this in mind when trying to determine which end to finish on, but remember the most important thing is to finish at an end. Go for the end.

4

Mental attitude

I heard a story once about two Flying Dutchman sailors who were racing in the United States Olympic trials. They were tied for the lead going into the next-to-last race and the two of them were first and second beating toward the finish. One boat tacked on the lee bow of the other about three boat lengths in front and one boat length to leeward. The crew ahead had the boat behind locked into a controllable position, but were a little nervous about how they were going and every few seconds the skipper would turn around and look at the second boat. The skipper of the second boat took advantage of this nervousness to play a little game with the first boat and what happened went like this: each time the skipper of boat number one turned around to look at boat number two, the skipper of boat two would head up slightly, making it appear to the skipper of boat one that they were pointing higher. So skipper one started to point higher also. Each time he turned around the boat behind seemed to be pointing a little higher than they were. When he turned back the boat behind would drive off and sail fast. Soon boat one had been pinched and pinched, and ended up going sideways. The boat behind caught up and eventually ground over the top of them.

Now, these two boats had been together the whole race and had almost identical boat speed. But all of a sudden because of a perceived disadvantage, the first boat began to go slower than its rival, simply because it was being *sailed* slower.

I remember another situation where I was racing in the 1979 Laser European Championship. I was coming up to the finish line in seventh place. The person in sixth place was about 50 yards ahead of me and we were two-thirds up the last beat to the finish line. There was no one close behind me. I was rather sceptical as to whether or not I'd be able to catch up to boat number six at all, but I decided what the heck, I would start trying. So I worked my way to the middle of the course with boat six tacking to cover. Once in the middle, I began tacking every 20 or 30 seconds. Boat number six, having quite a distance between himself and boat number five, elected to continue to

58

cover me each time I tacked. I played the shifts a little bit better than he did as he was sailing in headers a little longer, waiting to tack on me, and I soon began to catch up to him slightly. He got a little nervous and started tacking a little bit more directly in my wind. I began to tack a bit more often, maybe once every 15 seconds. We tacked and tacked and he kept watching me after each tack; he was beginning to get really nervous, so I started tacking even more, maybe once every ten seconds. We tacked a few more times and he was still about 30 yards ahead of me. Just before the finish line I saw that a gust of about 20 knots was about to reach him. I tacked and as he tacked to cover the gust hit him. He wasn't ready and he tipped over. I sailed by and finished sixth and he ended up finishing eighth because the boats behind us had caught up.

Those are two examples of a skipper letting his mind wander off the main priorities and allowing himself to be psyched out. Had the Laser sailor merely kept a loose cover on me it would have been very difficult for me to grind down 50 yards in only a third of a beat, especially since it was my perception before we went out to the course that he was a better sailor than I was. So the mental workings of competitors on the race course can play a significant role in who finishes where on which day. A good positive, confident attitude can help any competitor to shun the fear of being passed by other boats and will allow him to carry out his game plan more effectively. But if a competitor is not very confident or is a bit nervous about his abilities, he's more apt to be defensive and be passed by the aggressive, offensive sailors.

One of the most important factors of being able to do well on the race course is an understanding of your abilities as opposed to the abilities of the people you're racing against. If you know that you have more experience and a better chance of doing well than the others on the course, you are more apt to feel comfortable about your ability and be comfortable with the decisions that you're making as you race around the course. On the other hand, if you feel you have less knowledge or experience or ability than the others you will often feel uncomfortable with your decisions and begin disbelieving what you have tried to establish as the proper way to win the race.

It's very easy when you're racing in a locale that is new to you or against people that you think are very good to find yourself on the opposite side of the course from many of the top competitors and get nervous about that. When nervousness causes you to reevaluate your strategy the mental struggle will cause too much stress and fatigue while you're racing. Using the other boats is important but should be kept aside from the mental processes of sailing your own race as much as possible. Other boats should be used to learn about what's happening on the course; but once you've established what you feel is a proper way of sailing your race, the fact that the other competitors are doing something different doesn't necessarily mean that they are right and you are wrong.

Consistency

The way I approach most any race or regatta is with a conservative attitude. I aim to be consistent throughout the series. I try very hard to stay toward the middle of the course unless I am absolutely positive that one side is very favored. I continually use the people sailing outside of me on either side of the course to learn about what's happening as I'm sailing up the leg. To be consistent you have to use the other sailors on the course. When one side looks good, even if that's the side opposite to your game plan's side of attack, it should be analyzed as to why it looks better. If it seems that one side of the course is going to be more advantageous as you get farther and farther up the leg an approach to that side of the course should probably be made. Without the other sailors on the course this learning procedure would be very, very difficult.

Consistency is obviously an important part of any race. A regatta full of third places is probably going to take the series away from someone who is continually getting firsts and tenths or twelfths. A consistent approach means taking risks that are smaller but have a better possibility of payoff. Going for a big gain means taking a big risk, which can also mean affording a big loss. The smaller the risk, the safer the return. The more time you have left in a race, the more you can afford to take the smaller risks, catching a few boats at a time. Then if the risk turns out to be against you or the outcome of the chance is negative, you won't have lost a large amount and you can come back later in the race.

Fatigue

One problem that Laser sailors have to combat is fatigue. The Laser is a very physical boat and you have to work hard to do well in a race. There's no substitute for getting out in the boat and getting yourself fit. But even fit people get tired and, especially if you're a little out of shape or haven't been sailing the boat much, it is very, very important to be able to deal with fatigue.

Before you go out you can do a lot to deal with fatigue in terms of diet, rest and exercise. Running or any exercise that builds up your endurance is a help although it won't build up the sailing muscles — only sailing will do that. Eat three meals a day for the week before a regatta, get plenty of rest, and don't stay up until three in the morning the night before the first race. If you're going to be on the water all day, a good breakfast is imperative. Possibly some sort of snack and/or drink should be taken out on the boat with you to give you energy between races and keep you going throughout the day.

Once you're on the course there are several things you can do to help yourself out in terms of fighting fatigue. One is stretching yourself in before the race. Often on the first beat people will experience a lot of pain or soreness in their legs, stomach, shoulders and arms. Much of this is just due to the fact that they haven't stretched in properly and is not really a fatigue symptom. When you get out to the course it's important to go upwind, especially when it's windy, partly to learn about the course, but also to practice your hiking. Hike hard, trim the sail several times, hold the mainsheet — don't use the cleat. Do everything you have to do during the race that would require physical effort and slowly stretch yourself in for the day. If you're particularly tight from the previous day's racing, it may be a good idea to stretch yourself on the deck of the boat inverting your legs as much as possible. Stretch and massage your arms so you won't get cramps quite as easily. Things like this can be done before the start and are very beneficial to helping you fight off the muscle fatigue that occurs during the race.

The most important fighter of fatigue is your mind. Keep thinking about racing, keep thinking about windshifts, other boats in the area, tactical situations and boat speed. Concentrate while you're sailing around the course. The longer you can force yourself to concentrate, the harder it will be for fatigue to overtake you and make you suffer discomfort and even poor finishes.

One of the biggest mistakes you can make is to tack because you're tired, rather than because it's time to tack. I've done it, and so has practically everyone I've talked to who's raced a physically demanding boat. Learn to sail the boat so that when you do start to hurt badly you know how to relax a little bit.

If you're tight a quick stretch before the start should help you to loosen up for the race.

Sit in, and keep the boat going almost as fast as it would otherwise be going — in heavy air this means learning how to play the mainsheet and keep the boat moving without having to hike extra hard. In medium wind it means sitting in for 20 or 30 seconds to let your muscles catch up to where your body has been. Make sure that you're doing this in a smooth spot rather than during a big chop, and when no other boats are in the immediate area that might roll over you and take your wind.

Motivation

On the whole it's better to stay near other boats while you're sailing around the course not only for consistency's sake (not letting your competition get away) but because when other boats are right around you, your tendency to try harder is much greater. The others keep you motivated. They keep you moving. And you've got an absolute standard to measure yourself against in terms of boat speed and tactical performance. When you make a mistake it's immediately apparent when other boats are around. When you're sailing off by yourself your mistakes or your boat speed problems may not be as apparent and you'll take away from your overall speed for a longer period of time than if you are near other competitors. It will also help combat fatigue since you will be thinking about the other boats and not about how much you hurt.

Comfort ashore

An important consideration to me at a regatta, especially a long one, is to be able to live comfortably while I'm there. Sleeping on the floor, sleeping in the car, even sleeping in a tent (especially if it's nasty weather), is not such a great way to spend a regatta week or long weekend if you're planning on doing well. Finding someone to stay with in a house or staying in a motel are much more suitable methods of bedding down for the time that you're in competition and will leave your body and mind rested and prepared for the day's activities. Also while you are racing it's just as important to have three meals a day and plenty of rest as it was when you were preparing for the regatta.

The 'fun' philosophy

While you're out on the course and racing, it's important to remember that you are there to race. But it's crucial to

remember also that you're there because you want to enjoy the race. You're there to have fun. None of us gets paid for going sailing, and it's not our livelihood. We do it as a recreation, so it's important to keep it in that perspective.

On the course we are all going for a certain amount of blood. We want to win. We want to do well, at least better than the last time we went racing. And there are several philosophies to help us do well. Personally, I am always trying to think of my racing as long term. Each regatta is a practice race for the next. That mental attitude helps me to relax while I'm sailing in a particular regatta. During the race I try to sail consistently, staying near the large groups of the fleet – not going off into a corner by myself, especially early in the series. Every start is played conservatively, trying to get a *good* start, not necessarily the *best* start. Every weather leg is sailed trying to beat as *many* boats as possible, not *every* boat. Leave your risk-taking for later in the race. You can also take more risks in the later races of a series than in the early ones if you're behind. For instance, more chances are apt to be taken to catch up if it is the last race of the series and you need to beat ten more boats than you are currently ahead of to win the regatta. Conversely, toward the end of a series in which you're happy with your position, a more conservative approach should be taken.

Rules and protests

Just a short word here on the rules. The racing rules are based on logic and can easily be interpreted through logic. Almost any situation on the race course can be thought about and the proper rule decided upon even without knowing the rules thoroughly. Boats coming from behind have to keep clear of boats ahead. Boats going around markers have the right of way over the boats that are catching up from behind. The only thing the rules really explain are definitions like mast abeam, starboard-port, windward-leeward, luffing, and specifics such as limits on rights. Many of the rules can be figured out logically but nothing substitutes for an exact knowledge of the rules. If you are in doubt as to whether you're correct in any situation it's better to avoid that situation. At least *avoid a collision* and get about your racing as quickly as possible after the incident. When you do have a collision, someone has to be thrown out, whether you protest, the other person protests or even a third party protests; and when it comes right down to percentages the chances are about fifty-fifty that it will be you that is thrown out, whether you think you are right or wrong. So if you hit

somebody or they hit you and you get into that protest room, you've got just as much a chance of being thrown out in almost every situation on the course as they do. That's scary! But that's the way protests seem to work. Avoid those collisions!

Laser racing can be an exciting way to enjoy yourself on the water. I hope that through this book I've made this sometimes complicated sport a little easier to understand and enjoy.

THE INTERNATIONAL LASER CLASS ASSOCIATION

Laser sailing is not just about going for a sail on your local stretch of water. It's also about becoming part of a worldwide group of people with similar interests. For me the enjoyment of Laser sailing has been enhanced by membership of the International Laser Class Association (ILCA).

ILCA represents the interests of Laser sailors in the national and international governing bodies of sailing and with the manufacturer. It is the custodian of the class rules and constitution which protect the one-design concept of the Laser and the administration of the class. It organizes regattas, championships and training events, in fact anything to further the enjoyment of Laser sailing. Its work includes the publication of an international magazine and many national newsletters and bulletins, all of which keep you up to date with the activities of the class and provide you with tips on all aspects of Laser sailing.

I have been a member of ILCA ever since I started Laser sailing and for the small annual fee payable believe it to be excellent value for money. I would strongly recommend membership to all Laser owners! Application forms for membership are available from:

International Laser Class Association
Kernick Road Industrial Estate
Penryn, Cornwall TR10 9EP
England

or for North American sailors from:

International Laser Class Association
North American Regional Office
550 Delmar Road
Pointe Claire, Quebec H9R 4A6
Canada.